Where Is Hope?

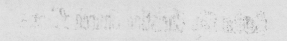

Where Is Hope?

PAUL CEDAR

MULTNOMAH

Portland, Oregon 97266

Excerpt in chapter 3 used by permission from Norman Cousins, "Hope Can Make You Well," *Parade*, 29 October 1989.

Cover design by Bruce DeRoos
Edited by Larry Libby

WHERE IS HOPE?
© 1992 by Paul Cedar
Published by Multnomah Press
10209 SE Division Street
Portland, Oregon 97266

Multnomah Press is a ministry of
Multnomah School of the Bible
8435 NE Glisan Street
Portland, Oregon 97220

Printed in 1992 by South Sea Int'l Press Ltd, Hong Kong.

Library of Congress Cataloging-in-Publication Data

Cedar, Paul A., 1938-
    Where is hope? / Paul Cedar.
      p. cm.
    ISBN 0-88070-358-X
    1. Hope—Religious aspects—Christianity. I. Title.
BV4638.C43 1990   90-35423
234'.2—dc20   CIP

"Hope: To cherish a desire with expectation of fulfillment."
-Webster's Dictionary

*I*s there hope?

That's the question I asked myself several years ago after the doctor told us that our two-year-old daughter was going to die.

He was a renowned physician—the chief surgeon of one of the largest children's hospitals in the United States. He and his excellent staff had done all they could do. In addition, they had consulted by phone with several other leading pediatric surgeons throughout the United States and Canada.

The consensus was the same. Our daughter Deborah could not live. Four major surgeries had not helped her. In fact, they had compounded her problem. Her trachea was completely sealed with scar tissue. She could not breathe except through a tracheotomy. She could not speak. But, worst of all, she could not live!

"I'm sorry," the surgeon said to us gently. "We've done all we can do. We've done our best. But there is no hope for her recovery."

Those were chilling words for us. *There is no hope.*

But my wife and I aren't the only people who've had to deal with those words. Every minute of every day, scores of people around the world are confronted with the same dreadful message: "There is no hope."

"There is no hope for your marriage."

"There is no hope for you to recover from cancer."

"There is no hope for you to succeed in your job."

"There is no hope for your daughter to graduate."

"There is no hope for your son's drug addiction."

"There is no hope . . . no hope . . . no hope."

While the messages are varied, the bottom line is the same. "There is no hope" is like a death sentence. When we hear it, we want to deny it. Escape from it. Sometimes we feel like we just want to die.

Life without hope is like a beautiful flower cut off from the stem. Like a precious child who has nothing to eat. We cannot live very well or very long without hope. Without it, we shrivel and die.

That's how I felt the day our doctor told us our daughter was going to die, that there was no hope for her. I felt like I wanted to die! I didn't want to live without her. I felt so empty and helpless—and hopeless.

In my despair, I cried out, "IS THERE HOPE?"

I found hope that day.

So can you.

THERE IS HOPE.

"Hope is the greatest sustaining force in life."
-Unknown

teve needed hope. He was at the end of his rope—ready to give up.

For years he and his wife had shared dreams and plans for the future. They had worked diligently to save money for their retirement years.

They had many plans—exciting plans—like sailing to Hawaii on their own sailboat, and spending every fall season in New England, and living for at least one winter on the French Riviera. Their list went on and on. There were so many intriguing things to do, so many exotic places to explore together.

But then it happened. The impossible! Without any warning, his wife left him for another man. After thirty-four years of marriage and just as many years of working and planning and dreaming, she was gone. They were within just a few years of fulfilling their dreams, and she left him.

With her departure went Steve's deepest feelings of hope.

He was alone.

He felt so empty; his future seemed so hopeless; his dreams were shattered. He felt betrayed and angry and depressed and lonely. He was overcome with a sense of helplessness. He wanted to die.

One evening, he went to a crowded cafeteria for dinner. After standing in line for what seemed a life-time, he became increasingly frustrated when he couldn't find a place to sit. In desperation, he apolo-getically asked a lady who was sitting alone if he could share her table.

She graciously consented. For several minutes they said nothing to each other. Steve was both angry and embarrassed. Nothing seemed to be going right for him. Even the little things in his life weren't falling into place like they used to do.

He ate hurriedly, hardly tasting his meal. When he was finished, he thanked the woman for her kind-ness. She responded by breaking into tears! He was shocked. As they began to talk, he discovered she was as lonely as he was. Her husband had died sud-denly a few months earlier. They had recently moved to the city. She didn't know anyone. She had no family. She was alone—very alone.

They sat and talked until closing time. Then they found an all night coffee shop and continued their conversation until early morning. As Steve drove home in the predawn darkness, he noticed he was feeling better than he had for a long time. For the first time in many months, he sensed there might be some hope for his future.

That feeling grew over the next weeks as he and his new friend spent more and more time together. Soon

they were talking about dreams and possibilities for the future. Six months after they met, they were married.

Steve not only found a wonderful wife, he had also discovered an important truth about hope: Hope does not need to be lost forever. Hope is always available for those who seek it.

That's a great story, you may be thinking, *but it sounds like a fairy tale. Nothing like that can ever happen to me. My situation is hopeless!*

If so, you are not the only one who has felt that way. I've been there myself. In fact, many people are convinced their lives are hopeless. As a New York taxi driver put it, "Life is a big fake. . . . We're just here to die."

I sympathize with anyone who feels that way, but the cabbie's statement isn't true. Life doesn't have to be a "big fake." We don't need to become fatalistic. We don't have to give up.

Even when we lose hope, it can spring anew. As Steve discovered, one of the ways we can experience authentic hope is by inviting a significant person into our lives. Renewed hope will frequently come with that person.

It's wonderful when a significant person brings hope into another's life. However, such a person is not the only source of hope available to us. There are yet other sources of hope. Please read on, because . . .

THERE IS HOPE.

3

*"Hope, of all ills that men endure,
the only cheap and universal cure."*
-Abraham Cowley

ope can make a big difference in our lives—even to
our health!

Dr. Rusty Lynn of the Whitman-Walker Clinic in
Washington, D.C., believes hope is an indispensable
element for AIDS patients. He has discovered that
"treatment of people with potentially fatal diseases is
useless if they don't have hope."

Norman Cousins agrees. He believes hope can even
help make us well. His study has focused upon how
hope can help those diagnosed with incurable cancer.
He relates the following story as a case in point:

> The scene is the recovery room adjacent to
> surgery in a Los Angeles hospital. The patient,
> a seventeen-year-old boy, has just been
> wheeled into the room following surgery for
> brain cancer. His father, a physician himself, is
> at his son's bedside.

> The surgeon comes through the door. He
> spreads his hands and says to the anxious

father, "We couldn't get it all out. It's very deep. It's no use. He's not going to make it. Maybe your son has a week to go. Ten days at most. I'm dreadfully sorry."

Suddenly the father hears sobbing sounds coming from the direction of the boy's bed. He realizes that his son is conscious and has overheard the surgeon. He sits down at the bedside and puts a hand on the boy's shoulder.

"Look, Son," the father says, "I don't believe him, and neither should you. I've seen too many people come through who were told they couldn't make it. Please believe me, Son. No doctor really knows enough to make that kind of prediction."

Cousins reported that story some six years after the surgery took place. The young man was still alive and in complete remission. Why did he survive? Without a doubt, the attitude of hope shared by both father and son made the difference.

Physicians and psychiatrists cannot fully explain the phenomenon. It relates to a new branch of medicine called *psychoneuroimmunology*, which deals with the interactions between the brain, the endocrine system, and the immune system.

Cousins concludes,

Intense determination and hope can have a physiological effect. Positive feelings, studies show, actually can stimulate the spleen, producing an increase in red blood cells and a corresponding increase in the number of cancer-fighting cells. These cells can destroy the cancer cells one by one, leaving normal tissue untouched—unlike chemotherapy which cannot distinguish between normal and malignant cells.

The bottom line is that hope can make a big difference to a person's health and well-being. In fact, sometimes hope can be the very factor which determines whether a person lives or dies.

Am I implying that hope is the solution to every dark situation, or that hope can overcome every obstacle we face? Of course not. But I am saying that hope can make a significant difference for good. Sometimes it can even mean the difference between life and death.

Of course, there is such a thing as "false hope." That's the kind of hope based upon things or persons which are fallible. That kind of hope will usually fail us.

In a sense, that was the problem Steve faced. He put his hope in a wife who was very much a fallible person. It was good for him to love and cherish her. But it was foolish for him to allow his life and happiness to totally depend upon her. When she left him, his hopes and dreams were dashed.

Authentic hope does not make us overly dependent upon people or positions or material possessions or anything that is temporary.

Although some of those things may enhance the quality of our lives, they are not enough. We need the kind of hope that will transcend the temporary. We need the kind of hope that will endure loss, overcome challenges, and enrich our lives.

That quality of hope is available to all of us.

THERE IS HOPE.

4

*"Everything that is done in the world
is done by hope."*
-Martin Luther

any people think the goal of
life is to make lots of money
or to hold an important posi-
tion or to accrue many material possessions. Most of
those people who have sought these, thinking they
would bring fulfillment, have been bitterly disappointed.

David was such a person. He was a distinguished
businessman who came to me several years ago for
counsel. Although he had been enormously successful, he was in deep despair. He'd tried everything he
knew to do, but his life felt utterly empty. He had the
terrible feeling he was slipping backward into some
kind of abyss. His situation seemed hopeless.

From the time David was a teenager, his goal in life
was to be successful. To him that meant making a
great deal of money, having a beautiful wife, living in
the largest, most lavish house in the city, being a community leader, and belonging to the best country club.

After graduating from high school, he received a
scholarship to one of the outstanding universities in
the nation where he became a student leader and a

successful football player. During his senior year, he married one of the most beautiful girls on campus.

When his studies were completed, he took a position with a national corporation. Within a few years, he worked his way up the corporate ladder. Many of his dreams were fulfilled. He was making a great deal of money; he and his family were living in one of the most beautiful houses in the city; he belonged to a fine country club; and he seemed to be able to buy everything he wanted. Yet his life felt incredibly hollow.

Deciding he needed to be involved in his own business, David resigned from his prominent position and launched out on his own. It seemed that he had the Midas touch. Everything he did succeeded. He made more and more money and owned more and more things. He and his wife began to travel to faraway places. They were able to do everything they wanted to do—and yet his life was not fulfilled. He felt overcome by hopelessness.

That's when he came to me. He thought I might be able to resolve his problem for him. "I've achieved everything that I hoped for," he told me. "I've been successful in my business, I've become an outstanding community leader, I've received every community award that I know about. I have a wonderful wife and three marvelous children, and yet I don't feel fulfilled. What in the world is wrong with me?"

His hopes turned out to be "false hopes." He'd achieved all of them, but wasn't fulfilled in the way he expected to be. Now he wanted to find the secret of authentic hope. He wanted to be fulfilled in a way that he was not. He was hurting so deeply that he

wasn't certain whether he wanted to live or die.

David put his trust and hope into what we may call the "temporary" things of life. Houses, clothes, bank accounts, BMWs, and businesses are temporary things. They simply don't last. Of course, he wasn't the first person in history to discover that truth.

Centuries ago, a man named Job had a similar experience. He was also an exceedingly successful and wealthy man. But in a matter of hours, he lost his children, his houses, his barns, his wealth, and even his health.

As he tried to recover from it all and to make sense of it, his wife and his friends attempted to encourage him. Instead of helping him, however, they compounded his problems. They increased his pain greatly. They were sincere in wanting to help him, but they were sincerely wrong in what they said and did.

Finally, his wife gave up hope. She told him to "curse God and die." Then she left him. Before long, his friends also gave up on him. He was all alone. He had no place to go and no one to turn to—until he looked up. Then he found hope.

My friend David had a similar experience. He had been hoping in the wrong things. He had lost his perspective. Even when his life was "full" with all of his achievements and possessions, he felt empty.

David needed more than possessions and achievements—and so do we. There was hope for Job, there was hope for David, and there is hope for us.

THERE IS HOPE.

5

*"Hope, like the gleaming taper's light,
Adorns and cheers our way."*
-Oliver Goldsmith

 everal years ago, I visited the infamous Berlin Wall for the first time. It was more ghastly than I ever imagined. Through my binoculars I could see heavily-armed guards on the other side of a bleak no-man's-land. I recalled dreadful stories about border guards gunning down anyone who tried to clamber over the wall and escape.

The wall looked impregnable. The thought of living long enough to see it come down seemed absurd, and the people with whom I visited in West Berlin agreed. They wanted to see the wall come down in their lifetime, but didn't expect it to happen. It seemed a foolish hope.

A few hours later, I traveled into East Berlin to spend several days in Eastern Europe. I visited with many people and found that most of them believed the wall would always remain. Although a few were hoping and praying the wall would come down, most believed no one could do anything about it. It was simply hopeless.

Just two years later, however, I sat watching live coverage of thousands of joyful celebrants pouring through fresh openings in the wall. The impossible was taking place. The walls were tumbling down! The impregnable Berlin Wall was opening before our very eyes. Hope was becoming a reality.

That's what authentic hope is all about. All of us long for our hopes to become reality. We want our prayers to be answered. We all have the ability to hope and pray—even when the situation seems hopeless.

That kind of hope is sometimes referred to as "hope against hope." Webster defines "hope against hope" as this: "to hope without any basis for expecting fulfillment."

Some people consider that kind of hope useless. Even stupid. The people of Berlin do not—nor did the valiant Minute Men of the American Revolution who won an impossible war—nor did the young athletes on the 1980 U.S. Olympic hockey team who captured an unlikely gold medal. Nor do I.

Again and again I've found that "hope against hope" leads to the fulfillment of my dreams. Norman Cousin's story of the doctor's son is an example. Over the years, I have seen many people experience the impossible. They've dreamed and they've prayed and they've worked—and the impossible has come true.

It's sad to see people mired in a lifestyle of hopelessness and despair. In contrast, it's exciting to watch people living with hope—even against what seem to be impossible odds. Living with hope is enjoying life at its best.

But where do we get hope? How can we find it?

Sometimes we find hope in the least expected places. That was true of Chuck Colson.

Colson was once one of the most powerful and influential men in the United States. His office adjoined the Oval Office of the President of the United States. He served as one of President Richard Nixon's closest associates and advisors.

Then the Watergate scandal erupted. Colson was one of the high government officials who was convicted and sentenced to prison. It was a difficult, humiliating time for Colson and his family. A time of despair and hopelessness.

Yet it was in prison that Chuck Colson found hope. His life was radically changed for the good. When he was released from prison, he began a significant outreach to prisoners. He is committed to help others find hope in the way he himself did.

Hope can be found anywhere—in prison, in the midst of broken relationships, in the environment of failure, or in the ecstasy of success. Authentic hope can be found in any situation at any time in any place. Hope is available to all of us all of the time.

My wife and I found hope in our impossible situation. When the doctors said there was no hope for our daughter Debbie, God gave us hope. And after years of multiple surgeries, Debbie is enjoying a happy and fulfilling life, and we are rejoicing.

There is hope. However you may be feeling or whatever you may be experiencing. Regardless of how hopeless things may appear, or how impossible circumstances may seem—I have good news for you.

THERE IS HOPE.

6

"Hope is brightest when it dawns from fears."
-Sir Walter Scott

evi Brown was born on the wrong side of the tracks. He never knew his father and remembers seeing his mother only a few times. By the time he was in high school, he had lived in twenty-three foster homes.

Levi had jumped from school to school. He hadn't learned to read. He believed he was stupid, and was embarrassed and fearful that someone would find out. So he held people off at arms length.

When he was eighteen, he dropped out of school. He was living in the inner city. He couldn't find any employment, but he did find a bunch of guys to hang out with. They formed a gang. For the first time in his life, he had the sense of belonging.

He was big and strong and a great street fighter. Before long, he became the second in command of his gang. He felt important. He had made something out of himself. He wasn't a failure. He and the other gang members became proficient thieves. Things were going well for Levi.

But then the inevitable happened. They stole a car and were caught by the police. Levi was sentenced to three years in the state penitentiary.

He was released after two years for good behavior. But within six months, he was caught breaking into a store. His next sentence was for five years. That became the pattern of his life. He was in and out of prison repeatedly. His life became more and more hopeless.

I met Levi when he was forty-two-years-old. By that time, he couldn't remember the number of times he had been in and out of prison. He was living on the street. He approached me as I was filling my car with gasoline at a service station.

He asked for some money for food. We began to talk and I found out he had no place to live. He looked hopeless and hapless. I was touched by his needs.

I encouraged him to go to a nearby shelter for men. There he could get food, a shower, and some clean clothes. And if he would agree to the rules of the house, he could stay there while he was looking for a job.

He agreed to give it a try. I checked in with him a few days later and found out he was getting along very well. He was enjoying the security of a home even though he was required to attend a daily Bible study and to help with the dishes after two of the daily meals.

Before long, he found out the shelter offered tutoring for those who would like to learn to read. It didn't take long to realize that he wasn't stupid at all. He *could* learn to read. Levi was as proud as a little boy.

The people at the shelter were good to him. He

sensed they loved him. At first he didn't know how to respond. He couldn't remember ever being loved by anyone.

In addition to his reading class, the shelter leader helped him enroll in an auto mechanics night class being offered by the city. Within six months, he was able to find a job. For the first time in his life, he was able to support himself.

In less than a year, Levi had moved from a place of total hopelessness to a position of authentic hope, from a life of fear to a life of love, from darkness to light. Life had never looked so good. There had never been so many possibilities.

Levi had been blessed by people who wanted to help him with no strings attached. They didn't exploit him nor take advantage of him. Instead, they simply loved him and helped him. And he responded with a full heart.

The story of Levi may sound too good to be true. But it isn't. In fact, these kinds of stories are taking place every day. No one should have to live without hope. No one should be alone. Every person matters.

There is hope in every situation. It may not always be easy to find, but it is available somewhere if we just don't give up.

When things look hopeless, it is not the time to give up. We need to keep looking, to keep knocking, to keep searching. There is hope out there somewhere.

In the midst of all of his problems, Levi learned one of life's most important principles. It is a principle which everyone of us needs to learn:

THERE IS HOPE.

> *"The best thing a psychiatrist can do for his patients is to light them a candle of hope to show them the possibilities that may become sound expectations."*
> *- Dr. Karl Menninger*

here are times when our lives become very dark and seemingly hopeless. We need to see through the darkness to the light of hope. It is always available for those who seek it. Hope can be the light that can touch our lives in any situation—even when darkness seems to overcome us.

Jonathan found that to be true. Although he was not nearly as successful as David, my businessman friend, Jonathan was suffering from the same kind of emptiness. He had a good job, an adequate house, and a fine family. Yet he found himself on the verge of losing everything and everyone that was meaningful to him.

For some eleven years, he had placed his hope in alcohol and drugs. More and more of his time and money focused on his addiction to those chemicals. He had become increasingly addicted. As he did, he became less and less effective in his work and more and more separated from his wife and children.

On a certain Friday, his employer gave him an

ultimatum: He either had to clean up his act or lose his job. That same weekend, his wife told him she couldn't tolerate his addiction any longer. She and the children were going to leave. Within an hour, they were gone.

That evening, he was alone and in deep despair. Hope seemed to have fled. He decided to kill himself. In a drunken stupor, he went to find his revolver. He sat down in a chair and checked out his gun. Everything looked fine.

Deliberately, he held the revolver to his head. He waited for a few seconds, then pulled the trigger. *Nothing.* Much to his surprise and despair, his gun wouldn't fire!

He checked it repeatedly and held it to his head again and again. But each time he did it, the gun refused to fire. It had always worked in the past, but regardless of what he did, he couldn't make the gun fire.

Finally, he threw it across the room in disgust. It hit the wall and fired harmlessly into the floor.

Jonathan broke into great sobs of frustration. He didn't seem able to do anything right. He couldn't even kill himself.

Suddenly, other thoughts found their way into his confused mind. *What if there is a God? What if God prevented me from killing myself? Could there be hope for me?*

He decided he had nothing to lose in trying to discover the answers to those questions. On Monday morning, he showed up at work totally sober. He informed his boss of his determination to remain sober and to get whatever help was necessary.

When he left his boss's office, he began immediately to look for Jerry, one of his colleagues. He had heard Jerry talk about God on several occasions. Until now, however, Jonathan had always scoffed.

He soon found Jerry and recounted his story to him. He needed help, and Jerry seemed to know something about God. Could Jerry help him get in touch with God? Could God help him overcome his problems?

Jerry took Jonathan to see a counselor. The counselor spent hours with Jonathan and then with his wife and children. Jonathan turned to God for help. His life turned around. His marriage was saved. His family was reunited.

Five years later, things are going better than ever. There've been some "slips" along the way, but Jonathan is a changed person. He found hope, and now he is actively involved in his church helping others to find hope.

This isn't an isolated story. There are hundreds and thousands of Jonathans in this world who are finding hope every day. And as they experience hope, they can share it with others. Hope can bring light into the darkest corners and the most forsaken areas of our lives.

THERE IS HOPE.

-8-

"When you say a situation or a person is hopeless, you are slamming the door in the face of God."
-Dr. Charles Allen

 man was dying.

It was a painful death—indescribably slow and torturous. He was being executed.

It was not his executioner's purpose to make his dying either quick or painless. They wanted his agony to extend just as long as possible and to be as excruciating as the most diabolical human mind could devise.

This execution was not to take place in private. This was a public event—a media event that even Hollywood or Las Vegas couldn't stage. Those present would not have been satisfied with seeing this spectacle on television—they wanted to witness it live and in color, not on the ten o'clock news.

The executors weren't the only persons present. A huge and noisy crowd of spectators huddled around. Thirsty for blood, they had whipped themselves into a state of frenzy. They loved to see such a man bleed and suffer and scream in pain. They wanted more blood and more guts and more anguish.

They showed no reverence for the dying man—nor did they display any compassion or even a hint of sympathy. They were loud and boisterous and obnoxious as they shouted insults and profanities at him. They mocked and ridiculed him. This was the best show in town—and they wanted to enjoy it to the full.

It's difficult to comprehend the pain the man was suffering—not only the physical torture and the mental agony, but also the *heartache*. Perhaps that was the most piercing and hurtful pain of all.

He was so alone! His mother and a few friends stood at a distance, but they were so engulfed in grief themselves they had little ability to encourage or help him.

But that wasn't the worst of it. Most of his friends had deserted him. When the authorities took him into custody, his friends scattered like frightened sheep. They were out to save their own skins. They were watching out for "number one."

In fact, when one of his closest friends had the opportunity to help him, he denied he even knew him. Then he ran for his life. This friend was big and strong with an awesome physique. He looked like he could have competed in a body building contest or played tackle for a professional football team. But he was a coward. He wanted to stay safe.

If that weren't enough, another of the dying man's most trusted friends had "turned him in" to the enemy, selling him out for just a few dollars. He didn't need the money, but he became his friend's Benedict Arnold.

And so an innocent man was dying—very much

alone. He had done the right things in his life; he had treated others well; he had been a loving and compassionate person. In fact, during his mockery of a trial, no one could agree on what laws he had broken. So they told lies about him. Everyone knew they were lies, but it didn't matter. They had decided they wanted to get rid of him. They wanted him dead once and for all.

His situation was hopeless! There was no remedy for his plight. No gallant knight would come riding into the scene on a white horse to whisk him away to safety.

There was only blood and suffering and violence and evil and mockery and hatred and injustice and aloneness. Above all, there was hopelessness.

Then he died.

THE END

"To the voices of hope that are calling you,
Open the door of your heart."
-Edward Everett Hale

r was it "the end?"

Could there be hope in even the most hopeless situation? Is there a way to escape the fear and despair and hopelessness of death itself?

IS THERE HOPE?

My wife and I, Steve, David, Levi Brown, Jonathan, and even Charles Colson found hope in difficult situations. Each of us had one common denominator in our experience—we turned to God. He brought hope to each of us—and he can do the same for you.

When we open the door of our hearts to God, he can bring hope into any and every situation. There is hope available to all of us all the time.

In fact, there was hope even for the family members and friends of the man who died such a terrible and painful death. His unjust execution was not the end of his story.

Three days after his death, some of his friends came out of hiding. They went to his grave early in the morning to take care of some burial details and to

pay respect to his memory. They went with heavy hearts and tears and guilt—and a deep sense of hope-lessness.

They weren't prepared for what they found.

His grave was open—and empty. Apparently, someone had stolen the body. He was gone!

The grief and tears turned hurriedly into anger and outrage. Who could have done such a thing? Who would be so evil as to desecrate the mangled body of a tortured man?

Then they saw a man nearby. They assumed he was an employee of the cemetery. Perhaps he could help. Maybe he could give them some clues as to where they could find the body of their friend.

They rushed to him. They began to plead for information . . . and then they stopped in their tracks. It was *impossible*! It couldn't be!

But it was. It was their friend. *He was alive!*

But that couldn't be possible! It must have been some kind of trickery or cruel joke. It couldn't be true. It had to be a Hollywood stunt or a spectacular illusion. It couldn't be real.

But it was. He was alive.

IT WAS JESUS!

Jesus said, "I am the resurrection and the life. He or she who believes in me, though they die, yet shall they live. They who believe in me shall have eternal life! Will you believe this?"

A paraphrase of John 11:25-26.

For God so loved the world that He gave His only son (to live and love and die and rise from the dead) that whoever would believe in Him would not perish, but have everlasting life.

A paraphrase of John 3:16.

THERE IS HOPE!

Will you believe this?